MADDIE
THE
MATHEMATICIAN
A CLOSER LOOK AT SHARING

WRITTEN BY NNENIA JOSEPH, Ph.D
ILLUSTRATED BY AL DANSO

Maddie
the
Mathematician

http://maddiethemathematician.com/
https://www.facebook.com/maddielovesmath/
http://about.me/nneniajoseph
nnenia.joseph@gmail.com

Printed in The United States of America.

Dedication

I would like to dedicate this book to my daughter Xenovia. I want her to know that mathematics is all around us and it has the potential to open many doors. Learning the language of math is the key to success. Remember not to let the challenges of mathematics prevent you from trying. I want you to continue to do your best and always think before you do.

Hi, I'm Maddie, and math is my thing!
If you like math, let me hear you sing.
One-Two-Three, math is for me;
Four-Five -Six, math's a quick fix;
Seven-Eight-Nine, we do it every time!
Next comes 10 and we can solve it again.
Now let's begin our math adventure!

Maddie loved sharing with her friends. This morning her mom made a batch of her award winning marshmallow chocolate chip cookies. Maddie smiled with excitement! She couldn't wait to take the cookies to school, so her friends could have a taste.

When she arrived, the class could smell the sweet chocolate marshmallow cookies as she entered the door. Everyone was gleaming with excitement. Even the class pest Samuel who never seemed to like anything wanted a taste of those cookies.

Ms. Burkett told the class that Maddie's cookies would be saved for snack time. When snack time arrived, everyone's mouth was watering.

When Ms. Burkett opened up Maddie's marshmallow chocolate chip cookies there was a huge surprise. Maddie's mother had only made a dozen cookies.

When Ms. Burkett saw this she told the class, "Oh! No, boys and girls, there is only one dozen cookies and we have 24 students, what are we to do?"

At first, the class did not see the problem.
Ms. Burkett asked, "One dozen cookies are a lot of
cookies, right?" Maddie raised her hand and asked
Ms. Burkett, "Aren't one dozen cookies enough?"

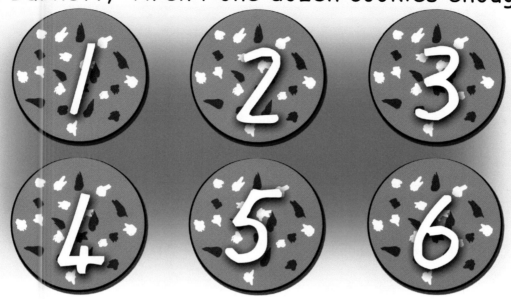

Ms. Burkett explained to Maddie and the class
that one dozen cookies were only 12 cookies.

She showed the class as they counted the cookies
together. "One-Two-Three -Four-Five-Six-
Seven-Eight-Nine-Ten-Eleven-Twelve."

As Maddie sprang to her feet, she yelled, "Oh! No, this is a problem!" Maddie counted the children in the class. There were 23 friends.

Maddie whispered to herself, "How is everyone going to get a marshmallow chocolate chip cookie?"

Maddie thought and thought . . . then suddenly smiled. She had a mathematical idea. Maddie noticed that the cookies were shaped like circles. At home, when she shared with her brother Michael, she gave him half of her cookie.

Maddie knew she could cut a circle in half and make two parts. "Ms. Burkett," said Maddie, smiling joyfully, "May I show the class my idea for solving the problem?"

Maddie approached the board and drew 12 circles, each about the size of an orange. She then drew a line through the middle of each circle. Once Maddie was done dividing the circles into halves, the class pest Samuel, said, "Oh! I get it." Samuel confidently walked to the board. He counted each half, in his screechy parrot voice.

"One-Two-Three-Four- Five-Six-Seven-Eight-Nine-Ten-Eleven-Twelve-Thirteen-Fourteen-Fifteen-Sixteen-Seventeen-Eighteen-Nineteen-Twenty-Twenty-one-Twenty- two-Twenty-three-Twenty-four!" The class all cheered! "We got it!" Maddie's math brain figured out that drawing a picture could help solve the problem.

Ms. Burkett was very happy with Maddie's mathematical thinking. She divided each marshmallow chocolate chip cookie in half and gave each class member one. She saved the last cookie for Maddie and handed it to her.

Maddie saw Samuel and divided the cookie in half. Samuel smiled and said, "Thank You". Maddie and her mathematical thinking saved the day!

About the Author

Nnenia Joseph (Hill) has been an educator for 12 years. She has first-hand knowledge of the difficulties children have with mathematics. In an effort to help her own daughter she created Maddie the Mathematician. She hopes Maddie helps children have fun with math and understand that mathematics is all around.

"Lifelong learning is the key to success and overall social development"- Nnenia Joseph

Maddiethemathematician.com

https://www.facebook.com/ maddielovesmath/

CPSIA information can be obtained at www.ICGtesting.com
Printed in the USA
BVIW12n0102131018
529214BV00015B/9

9 781936 937868